JUN 1 5 2011

DATE DUE

SEP 0 4 2012		
MAY 1 4 2014		

Demco, Inc. 38-293

A New Generation of Homosexuality: Modern Trends in Gay and Lesbian Communities

The Gallup's Guide to Modern Gay, Lesbian, & Transgender Lifestyle

BEING GAY, STAYING HEALTHY

COMING OUT:
TELLING FAMILY AND FRIENDS

FEELING WRONG IN YOUR OWN BODY:
UNDERSTANDING WHAT IT MEANS TO BE TRANSGENDER

GAY AND LESBIAN ROLE MODELS

GAY BELIEVERS:
HOMOSEXUALITY AND RELIGION

GAY ISSUES AND POLITICS:
MARRIAGE, THE MILITARY, & WORK PLACE DISCRIMINATION

GAYS AND MENTAL HEALTH:
FIGHTING DEPRESSION, SAYING NO TO SUICIDE

HOMOPHOBIA:
FROM SOCIAL STIGMA TO HATE CRIMES

HOMOSEXUALITY AROUND THE WORLD:
SAFE HAVENS, CULTURAL CHALLENGES

A NEW GENERATION OF HOMOSEXUALITY:
MODERN TRENDS IN GAY & LESBIAN COMMUNITIES

SMASHING THE STEREOTYPES:
WHAT DOES IT MEAN TO BE GAY,
LESBIAN, BISEXUAL, OR TRANSGENDER?

STATISTICAL TIMELINE AND OVERVIEW OF GAY LIFE

WHAT CAUSES SEXUAL ORIENTATION?
GENETICS, BIOLOGY, PSYCHOLOGY

GAY PEOPLE OF COLOR:
FACING PREJUDICES, FORGING IDENTITIES

GAY CHARACTERS IN THEATER, MOVIES, AND TELEVISION:
NEW ROLES, NEW ATTITUDES

**BLUE ISLAND
PUBLIC LIBRARY**

A New Generation of Homosexuality: Modern Trends in Gay and Lesbian Communities

by Bill Palmer

Mason Crest Publishers

Copyright © 2011 by Mason Crest Publishers. All rights reserved. No part of this publication may be reproduced or transmitted in any form or by any means, electronic or mechanical, including photocopying, recording, taping, or any information storage and retrieval system, without permission from the publisher.

MASON CREST PUBLISHERS INC.
370 Reed Road
Broomall, Pennsylvania 19008
(866)MCP-BOOK (toll free)
www.masoncrest.com

First Printing
9 8 7 6 5 4 3 2 1

Library of Congress Cataloging-in-Publication Data
Palmer, Bill, 1957-
  A new generation of homosexuality : modern trends in gay and lesbian communities / by Bill Palmer. — 1st ed.
      p. cm. — (The Gallup's guide to modern gay, lesbian, & transgender lifestyle)
  Includes bibliographical references and index.
  ISBN 978-1-4222-1754-2 (hardcover)   ISBN 978-1-4222-1758-0 (series)
  ISBN 978-1-4222-1873-0 (pbk.)   ISBN 978-1-4222-1863-1 (pbk. series)
  1. Homosexuality—Juvenile literature. 2. Lesbian community—Juvenile literature. 3. Gay men—Juvenile literature. I. Title.
  HQ76.26.P35 2011
  306.76'6—dc22
                              2010019195

Produced by Harding House Publishing Service, Inc.
www.hardinghousepages.com
Interior design by MK Bassett-Harvey.
Cover design by Torque Advertising + Design.
Printed in the USA by Bang Printing.

Contents

INTRODUCTION   6
1. GAY COMMUNITIES   9
2. THE FOUNDATIONS OF THE LGBT COMMUNITY   21
3. GAY LIBERATION AND AIDS   33
4. GOING MAINSTREAM   49
BIBLIOGRAPHY   61
INDEX   62
ABOUT THE AUTHOR AND THE CONSULTANT   64

PICTURE CREDITS

Biyahmadine, Nabil; Fotolia: p. 19
Buchalski, Frank; Creative Commons: p. 16
Creative Commons: p. 38
Dall'Orto, Giovanni; Creative Commons: p. 50
Freeland, Chris; Creative Commons: p. 29
Gryffindor, Creative Commons: p. 34
Icholakov, Fotolia: p. 11
Jensen, Derek; Creative Commons: p. 14
Jerici Cat; Creative Commons: p. 55
National Institutes of Health: p. 45
Pretzelpaws, Creative Commons: p. 57
Twin Cities IndyMedia: p. 46
U.S. Centers for Disease Control and Prevention: p. 42
U.S. Congress: p. 53
U.S. Department of Defense: p. 22
Zoe, Fotolia: p. 12

Introduction

We are both individuals and community members. Our differences define individuality; our commonalities create a community. Some differences, like the ability to run swiftly or to speak confidently, can make an individual stand out in a way that is viewed as beneficial by a community, while the group may frown upon others. Some of those differences may be difficult to hide (like skin color or physical disability), while others can be hidden (like religious views or sexual orientation). Moreover, what some communities or cultures deem as desirable differences, like thinness, is a negative quality in other contemporary communities. This is certainly the case with sexual orientation and gender identity, as explained in *Homosexuality Around the World*, one of the volumes in this book series.

Often, there is a tension between the individual (individual rights) and the community (common good). This is easily visible in everyday matters like the right to own land versus the common good of building roads. These cases sometimes result in community controversy and often are adjudicated by the courts.

An even more basic right than property ownership, however, is one's gender and sexuality. Does the right of gender expression trump the concerns and fears of a community or a family or a school? *Feeling Wrong in Your Own Body*, as the author of that volume suggests, means confronting, in the most personal way, the tension between individuality and community. And, while a community, family, and school have the right (and obligation) to protect its children, does the notion of property rights extend to controlling young adults' choice as to how they express themselves in terms of gender or sexuality?

Changes in how a community (or a majority of the community) thinks about an individual right or responsibility often precedes changes in the law enacted by legislatures or decided by courts. And for these changes to occur, individuals (sometimes working in small groups) often defied popular opinion, political pressure, or religious beliefs. Some of these trends are discussed in *A New Generation of Homosexuality*. Every generation (including yours!) stands on the accomplishments of our ancestors and in *Gay and Lesbian Role Models* you'll be reading about some of them.

One of the most pernicious aspects of discrimination on the basis of sexual orientation is that "homosexuality" is a stigma that can be hidden (see the volume about *Homophobia*). While some of my generation (I was your age in the early 1960s) think that life is so much easier being "queer" in the age of the Internet, Gay-Straight Alliances, and Ellen, in reality, being different in areas where difference matters is *always* difficult. Coming Out, as described in the volume of the same title, is always challenging—for both those who choose to come out and for the friends and family they trust with what was once a hidden truth. Being healthy means being honest—at least to yourself. Having supportive friends and family is most important, as explained in *Being Gay, Staying Healthy*.

Sometimes we create our own "families"—persons bound together by love and identity but not by name or bloodline. This is quite common in gay communities today as it was several generations ago. Forming families or small communities based on rejection by the larger community can also be a double-edged sword. While these can be positive, they may also turn into prisons of conformity. Does being lesbian, for example, mean everyone has short hair, hates men, and drives (or rides on) a motorcycle? *What Does It Mean to Be Gay, Lesbian, Bisexual, or Transgender?* "smashes" these and other stereotypes.

Another common misconception is that "all gay people are alike"—a classic example of a stereotypical statement. We may be drawn together because of a common prejudice or oppression, but we should not forfeit our individuality for the sake of the safety of a common identity, which is one of the challenges shown in *Gay People of Color: Facing Prejudices, Forging Identities*.

Coming out to who *you* are is just as important as having a group or "family" within which to safely come out. Becoming knowledgeable about these issues (through the books in this series and the other resources to which they will lead), feeling good about yourself, behaving safely, actively listening to others *and* to your inner spirit—all this will allow you to fulfill your promise and potential.

James T. Sears, PhD
Consultant

chapter 1
Gay Communities

When Mike was in his first year at the local community college, he announced to his family that he was gay. Luckily for him, his family was a loving and supportive one (and his father's favorite sister, June, was a very "*out*" lesbian). After graduation, he left his little Indiana town and moved into an apartment with a housemate near Wrigley Field in Chicago. Six months later, his younger sister Heather took the bus to the Big City to visit Mike for a long weekend. Even though they were seven years apart, they had always been close, and they were both anxious to spend some time together.

"Welcome to Boystown," Mike said with a grin when they got to his neighborhood. It had earned its nickname because of its popularity as a place for gay men to live.

What's That Mean?

A gay person who is *out* is someone who is open with other people about his or her lifestyle.

What's That Mean?

The *Rainbow Flag* is a symbol of gay pride and welcome.

Mike had planned a whole weekend of activities for them: a Cubs game with Mike's roommate (who had more cool piercings and tattoos than Heather had ever seen) and her girlfriend (who had even more!); a potluck dinner with the members of Mike's Gay Men's Chorus group; shopping (Mike bought Heather a tee-shirt with the words "Girl Pride" printed in glitter at a little shop on Broadway); services on Sunday morning at a church where they flew the **Rainbow Flag**, followed by brunch at a restaurant where their waitress was a tall, elegant African-American woman who called everyone "Sweet Thing" (and who Mike told Heather had been born a man). Heather and Mike had a wonderful time together!

Just before he put Heather on the bus back to Indiana, Mike asked her, "So, what do you think of my community?"

Heather thought for a moment about what this question meant. She thought of Mike's neighborhood, his housemate, his friends, his church, and his favorite restaurant. She thought of how nice everyone had been to her and how happy Mike was in Boystown.

"I love your community, Mike!" she said.

Mike gave Heather a big hug. "So do I, Little Sister!"

The Human Community

Human beings are social animals. Scientists tell us that our earliest ancestors, like many animal species, lived together in small groups of individuals, many of them related, who cooperated with each other for the common good of the group—protection from danger, cooperation in hunting and food-gathering activities, the sharing of that food, the care of the young. We needed each other to survive in the world, as we still do. Over time, people's concept of what defined their group grew larger to include their village,

Churches that fly the Rainbow Flag proclaim their willingness to welcome people from the LGBT community.

Gay Communities 11

their tribe, and eventually their nation. In the twenty-first century, many people think that the best hope for our future is to expand our understanding of our "group" to include all the people on the Earth.

As social animals, we live our entire lives among other people; we are happiest when our lives are rich with relationships, when we live in community. The word "community" may be a little hard to define sometimes, because it means different things to different people, but basically it refers to a group of people who are connected by bonds of respect, shared identity, and a shared sense of interests and

A community can mean different things, but it is always more than just a random group of people. Communities are connected to each other in some way—either because they live close together or because they share common interests or identities.

values. Often a community is thought to have a specific geographical location—a neighborhood, a town, a city—but that's not necessarily always the case.

We are born into certain communities that can be very important to our sense of **identity** as we grow up—our family, our **ethnic** or racial heritage, our religious tradition, our hometown, our nation. The traditions and **values** of these most basic communities shape our view of the world and who we are.

Throughout American history, ethnic and racial **minority** groups, especially those that have been the victims of prejudice and **oppression**, have formed and supported particularly strong communities. Native Americans, African-Americans, Hispanics, Jews, new immigrants (at various times the Irish, the Italians, the Chinese) have stuck close together to support each other economically and socially in

What's That Mean?

Identity refers to the way a person, or a group of people, define and understand who they are.

An **ethnic** group is a group of people defined by race, nationality, or language.

Values are shared rules and expectations for behavior.

A **minority** is a group of people within a larger group, usually differing in race, religion, or ethnicity from the majority.

Oppression is a system of social and legal restrictions that keeps a certain group of people in an inferior position.

tough times. These minority groups often chose—and were sometimes forced—to live in closely knit neighborhoods, keeping their traditions and their heritage alive as a matter of pride and group strength. These kinds of ethnic and racial communities still exist in many of America's town and cities; many are still facing economic and social disadvantages—and still finding strength in their community identity. Forming strong communities in the face of oppression is one of the great strengths of the human family.

For some people, the communities they choose to become a part of are as important, or more impor-

Minority groups often choose to live near each other to give support and identity to their communities. Chinatown in New York City is a good example of this.

tant, to them than the community into which they were born. These voluntary communities can also be powerful means of support, strength, and happiness for people.

An Invisible Minority

The situation for gay and lesbian people is somewhat unique. They are born and grow up in communities just like everybody else. But unfortunately some of these very communities that exist for the strength and happiness of its members—the family, the church, the ethnic group—are the very ones that have in the past rejected and excluded gay people, and unfortunately still do today. While society has been maturing in its attitudes toward **LGBT** people, mostly through the efforts of education and political action by LGBT people themselves, thousands and thousands of gay people have nevertheless been rejected by their families, by their church, and by the "values" of their hometowns.

But one of the great strengths of human beings is that even in the midst of oppression and rejection, people continue to seek each other out and build supportive communities for themselves, sometimes against great odds.

> **What's That Mean?**
>
> **LGBT** stands for lesbian, gay, bisexual, and transgender people.

Gay Communities 15

These rainbow markers identify the Boystown neighborhood in Chicago.

16   A New Generation of Homosexuality

The Williams Institute at the UCLA School of Law estimates that there are 8.8 million openly gay, lesbian, and bisexual people living in the United States.

> **EXTRA INFO**
> Boystown is the commonly used nickname for the East Lakeview neighborhood of Chicago. It is bordered by Lake Michigan on the east and Clark Street on the west, Irving Park Road to the north and Diversey Avenue to the south. Boystown gets its name because it has been home to many gay men since the 1960s.
>
> The two main (north-south) avenues of Halsted Street and Broadway are the heart of the neighborhood. Broadway is home to many different shops and businesses, while Halsted is the center of nightlife, with more than thirty gay and lesbian bars, nightclubs, and restaurants.

Various studies have estimated between one in ten and one in twenty people are "gay," but how the word is defined and how comfortable people are in identifying themselves with that word makes these estimates very approximate. What is clear is that there are many gay and lesbian people in our country, perhaps about the same number as there are left-handed people! And like left-handed people, gay people are born into all kinds of families in all kinds of places. Despite some people's **stereotypes**, you can't tell if people are gay just by looking at them. They are, in some ways, an invisible minority.

But "invisible" or not, gay and lesbian people have always found ways to locate each other and build their own communities. Many young gay people growing up thought they were the only "different" person in the whole world, and they suffered deeply by themselves. But discovering just one other gay person in their town (or sometimes even a character in a book or in a movie) began to open up a whole new world to them where they were not alone. A best friend with whom you can be honest, a few gay friends in your school, a trusted older gay relative: these can be the beginnings of a young person's gay community. Many people, like Mike in our story, have sought a larger gay community in the bigger towns and cities, and have found happiness and self-esteem by associating with large numbers of other gay and lesbian people.

Gay and lesbian people have been building communities in the midst of the oppressive society of the past, through the health crisis of the AIDS epidemic, and in these hap-

What's That Mean?

A *stereotype* is a picture we have in our heads about a group of people. It's not necessarily true. In fact, it seldom is, because people are individuals, and each person within a group is different.

For gay people, "finding each other" is not just about finding a partner; partners also need a larger community to support and understand them.

pier, but still challenging times of increasing rights and social acceptance for LGBT people. The Internet and the growth of social networks (Facebook, Twitter, etc.) has expanded membership in the larger gay community to people in rural areas, small towns, and around the world.

Gay and lesbian people, like other minority groups, have worked hard to build and strengthen their communities. In the twenty-first century, there is no longer any reason for LGBT people to feel they are alone in the world. The community is strong, and full of life and energy!

FIND OUT MORE ON THE INTERNET

Gay Community and Its Straight Neighbors
gawker.com/5511796/a-contract-between-the-gay-community-and-our-straight-neighbors

Lifecycle of an Ethnic Community www.jaha.org/edu/discovery_center/community/pdf/JHDC_life_before-wksht02.pdf

READ MORE ABOUT IT

Kompes, Gregory. *50 Fabulous Gay-Friendly Places to Live.* Franklin Lakes, N.J.: Career Press, 2005.

Mazziotti, Maria Gillian. *Growing Up Ethnic in America: Contemporary Fiction About Learning to be American.* New York: Penguin Press, 1999.

chapter 2
The Foundations of the LGBT Community

Ramona came from a close Mexican-American family in Fresno, California. Growing up in the 1930s, she always felt a little different from her sisters and the other girls in her town, but she tried to fit in and be the young lady her family wanted her to be. At seventeen, she and her brother's best friend, Miguel, became engaged to be married, but she was secretly relieved in 1942 when the war came, and Miguel joined the Navy. Although she tried so hard to be normal and prayed every day to change, Ramona had a very guilty secret: she liked girls.

With the war on and the men overseas, there were suddenly lots of jobs for women, and Ramona moved to Los Angeles to get a job at an airplane factory where her cousin Maria worked. Ramona loved the freedom of being away from her strict family,

During World War II, women had new opportunities, and they began to see themselves in a new way: as people who were strong and competent. These new attitudes also brought opportunities for the lesbian community.

22 A New Generation of Homosexuality

the independence of having her own money, and the little things, like being able to wear jeans and boots and keep her hair short the way she liked it. She lived in a rooming house with a lot of other girls from all over the country and, for the first time in her life, she met girls who liked other girls, just like she did.

They called themselves "the gay girls," and they were a close group. Some of the other women really didn't like them, though, and called them horrible names and sometimes even pushed them around. The "gay girls" always stuck up for each other, and Ramona learned she was pretty tough. One night at a bar, Ramona met Helen, a tall, beautiful blond woman from Texas. Within a few weeks, Ramona and Helen were a couple, very much in love. They talked about how they would save their money and buy a house together after the war and be together forever. One thing Ramona knew was that she was not ever going back to Fresno, and she was not going to marry Miguel. She was a gay girl.

Finding Each Other

Gay men and lesbians have always been able to find each other. The human need for companionship, both social and sexual, is so strong that even against the great odds of *oppression* and prejudice,

What's That Mean?

Oppression is a system of social and legal restrictions that keeps a certain group of people in an inferior position.

The Foundations of the LGBT Community　23

people find a way to connect. Gay people sometimes talk about "gaydar," the ability to recognize another gay person by a look, a gesture, or sometimes just a "sixth sense," and they have relied on that sense to meet each other in the most oppressive times and places.

Gathering places for gay men have been documented since ancient times. The public baths and gymnasiums of Ancient Rome were well known as places for gay men to meet and socialize. Throughout history, gay men have had the opportunity to meet each other, although often secretly, through traditional all-male organizations such as sports clubs, fraternities, schools, and the military. Neighborhoods in Amsterdam and London as far back as the 1600s were know for their taverns and coffee houses that were friendly to men who were homosexuals. These men used a special slang as a kind of secret code among themselves to identify each other while remaining hidden from the outside world. The word "gay" itself, meaning a homosexual person, may have had its origin in the homosexual slang of the 1700s. Slang, secret symbols, and **nonverbal** communication were all a part of the identity of older gay communities.

The early history of anything like a lesbian community is harder to identify. For most of the past, women lived lives that were less public, more tied to the home and family, and less written about than the lives of men. However, throughout history, two women were often able to live together openly, since people around them would assume they were simply two lonely unmarried women, living together for protection and companionship.

For most gay people in the days before the **gay liberation** movement, their hometowns were difficult and often unhappy places to live. Small-town prejudices, family restrictions, and the judgment of the church kept them from pursuing happy and fulfilling lives for themselves. But some gay people looked for alternatives to the communities into which they were born.

The frontier of the American West in the 1800s, for example, opened up possibilities for gay people, especially men, to escape to a more open and free environment and lifestyle. The tradition of gay cowboys and their "pardners" goes back well before Brokeback Mountain. The growing cities of America also offered a certain amount of freedom to gay people. The seaport cities of New Orleans, San Francisco, and New York, with their ***transient*** populations of single people and

What's That Mean?

When something is *non-verbal*, it is communicated without the use of words.

Gay liberation is the movement for the civil and legal rights of gay people with origins in the late 1960s and '70s.

Transient refers to a lifestyle where people move from place to place without strong ties to home.

The Foundations of the LGBT Community

their open-minded traditions were especially attractive to gay people (and for many of the same reasons, they still are).

In the 1860s, the poet Walt Whitman wrote:

> Once I pass'd through a populous city imprinting my brain for future
> use with its shows, architecture, customs, traditions,
> Yet now of all that city I remember only a man I casually met
> there who detain'd me for love of me. . . .

But of course, few gay people were as freethinking and self-aware as Walt! Most gay people tried to live their lives as best they could in their hometowns, without any kind of gay community to support them.

A Changing World

World War II (1939–1945) brought enormous changes to American society, changes that laid the real foundations of what we call the LGBT community. Nearly every young man and many young women between the ages of eighteen and thirty left home to serve in the military, where they were exposed to the company of people from all kinds of backgrounds and from all parts of the country. Men from farms and small towns were suddenly experiencing what life was like in the big cities, women from "respectable, old-fashioned" families were making friends with "fast" girls who drank and smoked and never went to church. And with so many men in the Armed Forces, women in huge numbers left their traditional roles in the home to become factory workers in the booming war industry plants, which gave women economic and social opportunities they had never had before. While the Nazis were exterminating gay people in concentration camps in Europe, millions of gay people in America were discovering their own identities and meeting each other on a scale never before seen in history.

> **What's That Mean?**
>
> Something that is *conservative* resists change; it is not open to new ideas.
>
> A neighborhood that is *bohemian* is one where the residents are nontraditional in their lifestyle and often interested in the arts and political movements.

After the war, most gay and lesbian people went back home to their **conservative** and disapproving communities. But some never did. Large numbers of gay ex-servicemen and gay women, liberated from traditional roles by war work, settled in the low-rent **bohemian** neighborhoods of the big seaport cities, attracted to the freedom and openness they found there. Neighborhoods like the French Quarter in New Orleans, Greenwich Village in New York, and the Castro District in San Francisco were magnets for gay people from all over the country in the post-war

What's That Mean?

Pioneers are people who are the first to try new things and experiment with new ways of life.

years. And it was in the cities of America in the 1950s and '60s that the gay community was born.

Bar Communities

Still lacking legal rights and facing societal prejudices, even the urban **pioneers** of the LGBT community were forced to hide their homosexual identities in all but a few select places. Across America, bars and nightclubs were the only possible comfortable, indoor meeting places for most gay and lesbian people. These bars were often owned by

EXTRA INFO

The aftermath of a bar raid at the Stonewall Inn in Greenwich Village in June 1969 gave birth to the modern gay liberation movement. On that hot summer night, gay people resisted the police and stood up for their rights, refusing arrest and rioting in the streets.

organized crime figures who took advantage of their gay customers by charging high prices for admission and drinks. Bar owners often paid off the local police in order to offer their customers some protection

28   A New Generation of Homosexuality

from legal harassment. One lesbian woman from New Orleans, now in her eighties, recalls that in the 1950s, "they would flash a light on the dance floor when the police were on the premises and we would all quickly change dance partners." Being caught dancing with another woman was against the law, and you could be arrested for it."

But despite these payoffs (and flashing lights), gay bars were subject to police raids at any time, raids where gay people would be arrested and their names printed in the newspaper. Being arrested in a raid,

Gay nightclubs have always been places where the LGBT community found each other

sometimes for simply having a quiet drink with your friends, destroyed many peoples' lives and careers.

Smaller cities often didn't even have a gay bar, but gay people developed strategies to meet each other in "regular" establishments. A retired gay professor in Binghamton, New York, remembers the early 1960s: "Thursday night was gay night at the Arlington Hotel Bar. If you wore a red tie, we gay guys would be able to recognize each other."

EXTRA INFO

Older lesbians sometimes joke that they always had an alternative to the bars. As one woman writes, "Joining a woman's softball team was often the first move a new lesbian in town made to meet like-minded women."

There were disadvantages, of course, to bars being the only meeting place for gay people. The bar culture encouraged heavy alcohol consumption, and the dollars gay customers spent often went into the pockets of criminals. And the bars were never really "safe."

Double Lives

The urban gay neighborhoods of the 1950s and sixties may have been places of relative safety and comfort, but police harassment and the very real

EXTRA INFO

The Daughters of Bilitis was one of the first lesbian social and political groups in the world. Meeting informally in the homes of its members as an alternative to the bars, the Daughters of Bilitis (or DOB) kept its membership list secret and urged its members to attend meetings in traditional feminine clothing so as to avoid harassment by the police (in the 1950s it was illegal for women to wear men's clothes in public). Membership grew over the years, and the DOB became a real force in advocating for gay people's acceptance in society through their biyearly conventions (starting in 1960) and their magazine The Ladder, published from 1956 to 1972. The group disbanded in the mid-1970s. On June 16, 2008, Del Martin and Phyllis Lyon, the founders of the DOB, were the first same-sex couple to be married legally in San Francisco. They had been in a committed relationship for fifty-six years.

threat of violence and exposure still haunted the gay people who lived there. Many gays lived what can only be called "double lives," forced to pretend to be straight at their jobs and with their families, only free to express their gay selves in the secret world of bars and clubs and on a few streets in their city.

In many ways, however, these big-city gay people were the lucky ones. In small towns and rural areas across America, most gay people had few opportunities to meet each other and many lived lonely, unhappy lives hiding their "dirty secret."

But against great odds, some gay and lesbian people were thinking about the larger issues of gay civil rights and the acceptance of gay people by society. As early as the 1950s, committed people—like the Mattachine Society in Los Angeles in 1950 and the Daughters of Bilitis in San Francisco in 1955—were forming political groups. And both the urban gay pioneer and the early gay political activist were very important in the development of the modern gay community, as would be the gay liberation movement and the AIDS crisis.

FIND OUT MORE ON THE INTERNET

The Castro District
www.sfgate.com/neighborhoods/sf/castro/

Lesbians in World War II
www.outhistory.org/wiki/Lesbians,_World_War_II_and_Beyond

READ MORE ABOUT IT

Chauncey, George. *Gay New York: Gender, Urban Culture, and the Making of the Gay Male World, 1890–1940.* New York: Basic Books, 1994.

Faderman, Lillian. *Odd Girls and Twilight Lovers: A History of Lesbian Life in Twentieth Century America.* New York: Columbia University Press, 1991.

chapter 3
Gay Liberation and AIDS

Frank left Georgia on his twenty-second birthday, May 14, 1977, and he never looked back. He had left a good job at his father's insurance agency, and his mother said he was breaking her heart—but he loved living in San Francisco. Even though he was not making much money working as a waiter ("wasting his education at the best Christian College in the South," his father said) and was living in a tiny apartment in a run-down neighborhood, Frank felt like the luckiest guy in the world as he dressed for his friend Steve's party.

He put a Village People record on the turntable and danced to "Macho Man" as he got ready, blow drying his hair, trimming his mustache, and laying out his Levis, his tightest tee shirt, his brand-new black leather bomber jacket. He was a little nervous since he knew there would be at least two of his old boyfriends at Steve's, but hey, he sure wasn't going to miss one of the hottest parties of the year. And

What's That Mean?

Something that is accepted, understood, and supported by the majority of people is said to be *mainstream*.

tomorrow was the Gay Pride Parade in the Castro District! Oh, if they could only see him now back in Decatur! It was great to be gay!

The Birth of Gay Civil Rights

The last forty years have seen an incredible transformation in LGBT communities, moving these communities out of the shadows and into the *mainstream* of American life. The struggle for LGBT rights and the huge challenges of the AIDS crisis were two of the major forces at work in defining gay identity, in strengthening communities, and in building understanding between straight and gay people.

Today, the Stonewall Inn remains a symbol of gay rights to the LGBT community.

In 1969, it was illegal for people of the same sex to dance with each other in a public place, to hold hands, or to wear clothes that were not considered "normal" for their sex. Undercover police would go into bars and clubs, observe these behaviors, and close the place down. The liquor was confiscated and, if you weren't lucky enough to slip out the back door, LGBT people were subject to arrest for "disorderly conduct" or "lewd behavior," and their names were listed in the newspaper. The average New York gay bar was raided once a month during the 1960s, and the authorities were constantly bullying gay people.

At 1:20 a.m. on June 28, 1969, the police raided the Stonewall Inn in Greenwich Village, New York City. But this night was different. Gathering on the street in front of the Stonewall, a group of angry people—including a number of transgender "drag queens" who had been particular victims of the police—refused to be bullied. Fights broke out between the police and the crowd, windows were broken, parking meters smashed, and many arrests were made in what became known as "The Stonewall Riots." The story made front-page news across the country. For several nights in a row, groups of young gay people marched through the streets of Greenwich Village expressing their anger and frustration.

Many historians consider the Stonewall Riots the beginning of the modern gay rights movement, one of several powerful **civil rights** movements of the 1960s and '70s that started among African-Americans. Within days of the Stonewall Riots, a new political action group was formed in New York. Unlike the more secretive names of earlier homosexual rights groups like the Mattachine Society and Daughters of Bilitis, this one came right out and proudly called itself the Gay Liberation Front.

Gay Pride marches were organized in New York, Chicago, and Los Angeles on June 28, 1970, the one-year anniversary of the Stonewall Riot, and by the following year, similar events took place in Boston, Dallas, Milwaukee, San Francisco, London, Paris, Berlin, and Stockholm. These marches were a call for the recognition of the gay community, a show of gay pride, and a demand for civil rights.

Many LGBT people became **politicized** in the 1970s, starting gay rights organizations and support groups in towns and cities and college campuses, expressing themselves in newly formed gay community newspapers and magazines, and in public marches and rallies. Gay people were coming out in huge numbers and urging other gay people to do the same thing.

What's That Mean?

The rights of a citizen to personal and political freedom under the law are known as *civil rights*.

A person who is *politicized* understands his or her rights and demands them through political action.

36   A New Generation of Homosexuality

Partying

After so many years of oppression and secrecy, it was a time of great excitement and freedom and pride for LGBT people. Young gay people flocked to the cities, bringing new energy to the older gay neighborhoods and establishing new ones. Bars and clubs (no longer controlled by organized crime but with proud gay owners) and gay-owned businesses thrived. To the beat of disco music, LGBT people danced (together!) in a celebration of fun and freedom—often under the influence of alcohol and drugs.

EXTRA INFO

Today there are literally thousands of Gay Pride parades and festivals in cities and towns across the world; for example, more than half a million people participate in the Gay and Lesbian Mardi Gras in Sydney, Australia, the largest gay pride event in the world. June is officially Gay Pride month in many places, honoring the movement that was born when that first group of LGBT people stood up to the police at the Stonewall Inn in 1969.

"It was one big party," says one gay man remembering the 1970s, "the biggest party you could imagine."

The capital of Gay America in the 1970s was the Castro Street neighborhood in San Francisco, "a city

Harvey Milk was the first openly gay person elected to a public office in the United States. Tragically, his prominence brought about his death.

38   A New Generation of Homosexuality

known for its freedom" according to a song by the Village People, a popular music group of the time. Packed into a few square blocks were thousands of young gay men, the so-called "Castro Clones" (the East Coast versions were the "Christopher Street Clones" in New York) in their uniform of Levis jeans, tight shirts, and black leather jackets. They rejected the old "sissy" stereotypes for gay men of the past, and boldly proclaimed their new image to the world.

With a growing presence and increasing voting power, gays in San Francisco began flexing their political muscle. It was in San Francisco in 1977 that Harvey Milk, the subject of the 2009 film *Milk*, was elected to the position of City Supervisor, the first openly gay person elected to public office in the United States. (Tragically, he was assassinated eleven months later by a deeply disturbed and prejudiced coworker in city government.)

In other American cities, gay people created their own local versions of the Castro, often moving into run-down inner-city areas, buying and fixing up inexpensive houses, and generally cleaning up the neighborhood in a process called "gentrification." At a time when many American cities were in serious decline, gay people brought a new energy and commitment to urban living that helped reverse a downward trend.

On college campuses across the country, gay and lesbian students came together for discussions (called "rap groups"), political action, and social activities. At many colleges the gay organization's dances were the most popular on campus, bringing gay and straight people together in a spirit of fun. Meanwhile, the media was catching on to the new visibility of the gay community, and gay and lesbian characters were regularly portrayed in movies and television—not without stereotypes, but at least right there in the open. In small towns and rural areas, media coverage of gay life was giving LGBT people a sense that there was a world out there for them, too.

What's That Mean?

Something that is *collective* forms a group, where the needs and desires of the group are considered.

Cooperative has to do with people working together rather than in competition with each other.

When an idea is taken to an extreme position it is said to be *radical*.

Lesbians in the 1970s

Sometimes frustrated by the continued dominance of men in the gay liberation movement, many gay women created their own communities in the seventies. Women communicated through their own publications with in-your-face names like Lesbians Fight Back, Sinister Women, and Salsa Soul Sisters/Third World Women's Gay-zette. Lesbians formed their own support groups and community centers, and they hung out together in their own bars and

40   A New Generation of Homosexuality

restaurants. Politics among gay women tended to be more **collective** and **cooperative** as they fought a double oppression both as women and as lesbians. Bringing a particularly **radical** approach to the growing women's liberation movement, some lesbians worked toward building a society completely separate from men and completely free of men's power and control.

During the 1970s, tennis player Billy Jean King was an outspoken advocate for women's equality. She was the first American athlete to openly admit to having a homosexual relationship. In 2009, President Barack Obama honored her with the Medal of Freedom for the work she has done advancing the lives of girls and women through physical activity.

The End of the Party

The 1970s were a time of incredible experimentation in lifestyle, politics, and identity formation for gay people. Out of the closet for the first time in large numbers, gays reinvented themselves free of society's stereotypes, creating their own new communities. And then disaster struck.

"AIDS ended the party," as the saying goes in the gay community. In the summer of 1981, an article

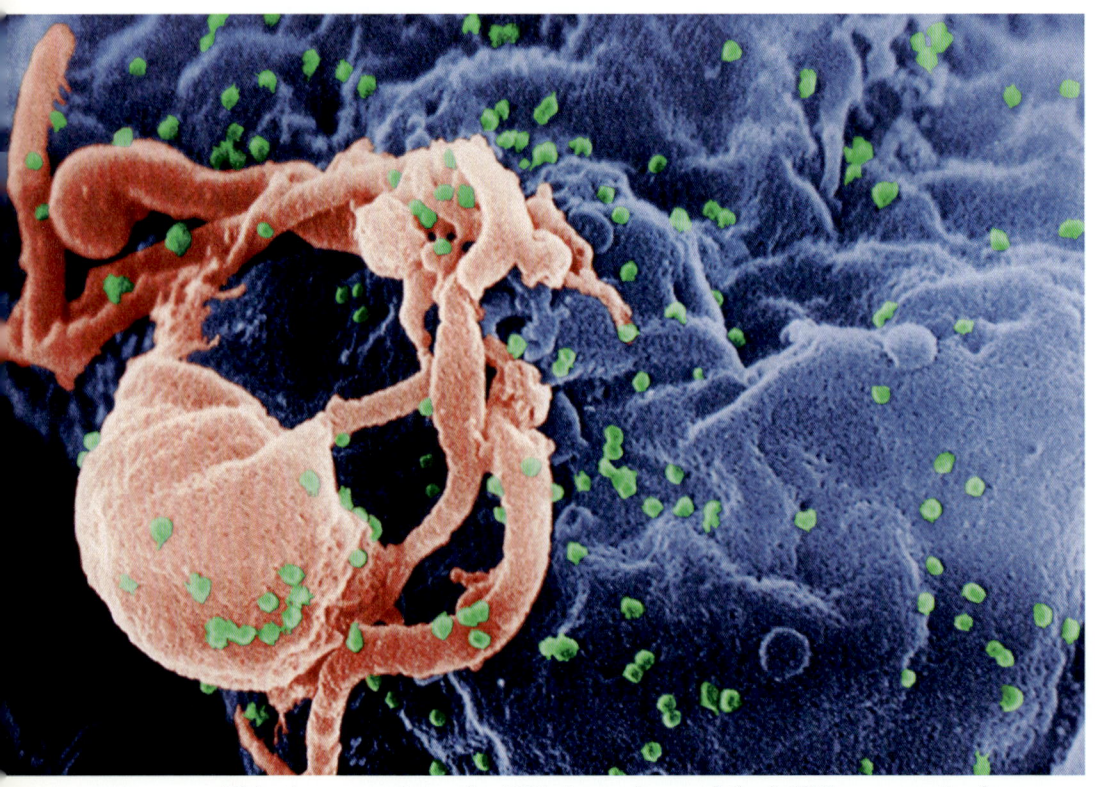

This tiny organism, the HIV virus, changed the LGBT community forever.

appeared in the New York Times about a mysterious new disease that was affecting gay men in New York and San Francisco. The symptoms were horrifying: skin cancers, infection, intense pain, pneumonia, death. Within months, dozens of gay men were sick and dying, and the gay community was terrified. Called "gay cancer," and later GRID (Gay-Related Immune Deficiency), it quickly became identified as a "gay" disease.

Without any known treatment and without any known cause, the medical care for these early victims of the disease was disgraceful. People lay in agony in hospital beds, covered in their own feces, while hospital staff, including even nurses and doctors, refused to enter their rooms for fear of catching AIDS. As the 1980s progressed, more and more gay men became sick and the death toll climbed. There were 16,000 reported AIDS cases by 1985.

"It seemed like overnight everyone I knew was getting sick," remembers a San Francisco man. "You'd run into guys on the street who six months before were the hottest men in the Castro . . . walking with canes and looking like skeletons. All I could think of was, was I next?"

Another recalls reading the obituaries in the newspaper first thing every morning and seeing the names of people he knew in what was chillingly called "the gay men's sports page."

EXTRA INFO

Frustrated and angered by the lack of government action in educating the general public about HIV/AIDS and in funding research and social programs, the AIDS Coalition to Unleash Power (ACT UP) was organized in 1987. The members of ACT UP were gay and proud and radical in their activities; they demanded that they be heard, they demanded that people with HIV/AIDS and their needs be taken seriously, they demanded that LGBT people have the same rights as any other citizen of the United States. They were committed to political action directed toward politicians and government agencies and to high-impact educational programs. More than twenty years later, they are still at it!

With the powerful **stigma** of having a "gay" disease, gay men with AIDS were the victims of tremendous prejudice. Sick people were evicted from their apartments, fired from their jobs, disowned by their families, and refused treatment by medical personnel. Since the general public believed the disease affected mostly gay men and drug addicts, it was slow to show any concern for people with AIDS, and the government dragged its feet for years in funding AIDS medical research and programs to

What's That Mean?

Stigma is a mark of shame.

44   A New Generation of Homosexuality

On the left is Dr. Robert C. Gallo, the researcher who told the world about HIV/AIDS. On the right is Dr. Albert B. Sabin, the discoverer of the polio vaccine. These two men show the power science has to touch human lives. The world waits in hope for the scientist who will discover a cure for HIV/AIDS.

EXTRA INFO

Gay community newspapers have been a very important way for LGBT people to stay informed of the news, events, and issues of importance to their community, especially in the days when "gay news" wasn't covered in the mainstream media.

The *Washington Blade* is the oldest LGBT newspaper in the United States and the second largest in circulation (the number of people who read it). Founded by a group of volunteers in 1969, the *Blade* is considered the most influential gay community newspaper in America because it reports local, national, and international gay news from the capital of political power, Washington, D.C., and is a source of news for people around the country. The paper has been published weekly on Fridays for over forty years. After a brief break in publication, the *Blade* resumed its important role in spring 2010.

help sick people. It seemed as if gay men with AIDS were being abandoned by society.

But their community did not abandon them.

Early in the AIDS **epidemic**, informal groups of friends—and, later, organized volunteers called "AIDS buddies"—helped to care for the sick men of the gay community. Cleaning apartments, walking dogs, grocery shopping, preparing meals, these buddies brought friendship and compassionate care to people who needed it. Despite their own health

ACT UP continues to be active as a force for bringing pressure on the government to fund AIDS research and treatment.

fears, AIDS buddies bravely faced the challenges of caring for their own people.

While government agencies and society in general stood by, gay people donated their own time and talent and money in the fight against AIDS and the care of those affected by AIDS. The Gay Men's Health Crisis (GMHC) was founded by a group of gay doctors and community leaders in New York City in January of 1982. It was the world's first, and it became the leading provider of HIV/AIDS education, prevention, and care.

What's That Mean?

An *epidemic* disease spreads quickly though an entire community.

Gay Liberation and AIDS   47

With advances in medical science and HIV/AIDS prevention education, AIDS is no longer the killer disease it once was in the gay men's community. It is today a treatable condition and a preventable one. But while it was raging in the gay community, it killed over 100,000 gay people, and the community has tragically lost a significant percentage of men who would now be in their forties, fifties, and sixties. Nevertheless, the modern gay community that was born in the gay liberation movement, and then was challenged and matured by the AIDS epidemic, came into the twenty-first century strong and proud and growing.

FIND OUT MORE ON THE INTERNET

Act Up
www.actupny.org/

History of the Castro District
www.sfgate.com/neighborhoods/sf/castro/

READ MORE ABOUT IT

Lyon, Maureen E. and Lawrence J. D'Angelo. *Teenagers, HIV, and AIDS: Insights from Youths Living with the Virus.* Westport, Conn.: Praeger, 2006.

Shilts, Randy. *The Mayor of Castro Street: The Life and Times of Harvey Milk.* New York: St. Martin's Press, 1982.

chapter 4
Going Mainstream

Cheri and Fran had been together for more than twenty years when same-sex marriage was legalized in Massachusetts. At Thanksgiving dinner in 2009, with their children Will and Eva and many friends and family present, they announced that they would be getting married that spring. Sixteen-year-old Will is the biological son of Fran and Tom, Cheri and Fran's best friend—nicknamed "Griz" because he is a big, gay Bear—while eleven-year-old Eva was adopted as a baby from China. Fran kept a blog for six months all about the wedding preparations, and Cheri was in constant contact with her Facebook friends the whole time.

The wedding took place on a beautiful May morning at Cheri and Fran's cottage in the Berkshire Mountains. Cheri's Aunt Betty, a Unitarian minister, performed the ceremony, which was attended by most of the members of Fran's Berkshire Women's Hiking Club, the Gay and Lesbian Families Organization of Western Massachusetts, the PTA of Eva's middle school, the Greenefield Gourmet Society, and many family and friends. At the wedding reception at the local Episcopal Church hall, Will texted to his friend Julie in Boston, whose two Dads had gotten married a few months before, "u are right! they do look like the two happiest women in America. but they wouldn't let me drink any champagne."

Gay couples have come out into the open—revealing to the world that gays are just ordinary people.

Gays Are Everywhere!

The gay community has gone mainstream in the twenty-first century. While still facing major challenges from conservative religious and political groups, the LGBT community has been growing in numbers, political power, and **visibility** as more and more gay people come out and claim their place in society. No longer a "hidden" minority, out LGBT people are everywhere—on TV, in movies, in almost everybody's family, in every town, in every school: everywhere.

And outside the big cities where the gay community first organized, gay and lesbian people are living proud, happy, and fulfilling lives in rural areas and small towns across America. Building on the foundations of the gay pioneers of the past, LGBT people today are enjoying a freedom and a sense of pride like they have never had before, despite still fighting a battle for civil rights and social acceptance that sometimes seems like it will never end. Gallup **polls** clearly show, however, that the majority of young people find LGBT lifestyles completely acceptable; a significant percentage of people under thirty fully

What's That Mean?

Something that is out in the open for the world to see has **visibility**.

Polls are scientifically gathered data on people's opinions.

Going Mainstream   51

approve of same-sex marriage and openly LGBT people serving in the military. Times are changing and are likely to continue to change as the older generation and the prejudices of the past lose their influence.

Getting to Know Each Other

Living proud and open lives, gay and lesbian people can serve as role models for each other and for the straight people in their lives, too. History has shown us that when people get to know each other on a personal level, as friends and coworkers and classmates, walls of misunderstanding and prejudice begin to crumble, and stereotypes lose their power. Real progress can be made in building strong, **diverse** communities when people learn to respect and understand each other, despite their differences. This is one of the most important lessons of all civil rights movements.

In cities and towns everywhere, LGBT people are active and valued members of their community. Since Harvey Milk's election to city supervisor in San Francisco in 1977, hundreds of openly gay and lesbian people have been elected to office at all levels of government, including people like Barney Frank, U.S. Senator from Massachusetts, and

What's That Mean?

A *diverse* community is made up of people from many different backgrounds.

52   A New Generation of Homosexuality

Barney Frank is an openly gay man who serves on the U.S. Senate.

Annise Parker, the Mayor of Houston, Texas. Openly gay and lesbian people contribute their talents and energy to their hometowns in all kinds of ways, serving on school boards, on church councils, as Little League coaches, and as volunteers in homeless shelters. In modern America, LGBT and straight people live and work side-by-side, they send their children to school together, they socialize together, and they belong to the same clubs and sports teams and community organizations. Gay people have become a part of just about everybody's everyday lives.

The Battle's Not Over

But LGBT people are still a minority group, and they are still fighting the battle for full social acceptance and civil rights that they have been fighting for decades. Gay political organizations and civil rights groups at the national, state, and local level are still very important to the LGBT movement. The Human Rights Campaign, headquartered in Washington, D.C., has over 750,000 members and supporters, and the organizing and fund-raising efforts of LGBT people in support of Barack Obama played no small part in electing the first African-American American president in history. Gay people vote for politicians who are responding to their concerns and issues, and politicians are learning to take those votes seriously. More and more Americans are coming to understand

There is even a "Gay Day" at Disney World!

that LGBT people deserve all of the same legal rights straight citizens enjoy.

Still Having Fun

And going mainstream doesn't mean that LGBT people don't still enjoy spending time with each other and the opportunity to be themselves in their own spaces! A quick glance at the listings in any gay community newspaper, like the *Vital VOICE* from Saint Louis, shows a community that likes to get together and have fun. There are clubs for gay men who play rugby and lesbians who ride mountain

EXTRA INFO

The International Gay Rugby Association and Board (IGRAB) is the organization for the world's gay rugby clubs. Based in London, England, it is dedicated to encouraging lesbians and gay men everywhere to play rugby. There are nearly fifty gay rugby clubs that are a part of IGRAB. According to their website, the goals of IGRAB are to:

- Lobby for the inclusion of rugby in the Gay Games and work with the Federation of Gay Games to foster rugby within the Games.
- Supervise a gay rugby world cup, known as the Mark Kendall Bingham Memorial Tournament, or Bingham Cup for short.
- Encourage the creation of more lesbian- and gay-friendly teams

IGRAB seeks to ensure that its activities and rugby in general are inclusive in nature. IGRAB will strive to ensure that no individual shall be excluded from participating in IGRAB or rugby on the basis of sexual orientation, gender, race, religion, nationality, ethnic origin, political beliefs, athletic ability, age, physical challenge, mental challenge, or health status.

bikes, for LGBT Catholics and Latino/Latina Youth, for gay families with children, for men who like to wrestle, and for women who like to read Jane Austen novels. Bars, coffee houses, and restaurants catering

The Bear community (a smaller community within the larger LGBT community) is made up gay men who are bigger, burlier, and hairier than the stereotypical image of a gay guy.

to the gay community do a thriving business, while LGBT people play and party together on gay cruises and at gay-friendly resorts in places like Key West, Florida, and the Russian River in California.

As more and more gay people have come out, the gay community itself has been learning just how diverse it really is. Many bigger, "furrier," traditionally masculine gay men have had a second coming out as Bears, a lively **subculture** within the community, with its own hangouts and recreational activities. The Rainbow Alliance of the Deaf has chapters all across the country. Gay teenagers and their friends meet through Gay-Straight Alliance clubs that have been organized in hundreds of high schools. And older LGBT people gather together at places like the Golden Rainbow Senior Center in Palm Springs, California. The gay community is a richly diverse one!

> **What's That Mean?**
>
> A *subculture* is a group of people with similar interests and lifestyle within a larger group.

The Internet, with social networking sites like Facebook and LGBT "cyber communities," is adding new life to the gay community as well. Gay people were pioneers in communicating with each other electronically. The Bear community, for example, organized and grew in the 1990s through the online

Bear Mailing List. LGBT people in small towns and rural areas discovered each other and their links to the larger gay community by visiting websites and making friends in chat rooms and by e-mail. And while young people have to be especially careful to protect their safety and identity online, some gay youth get needed support and encouragement from their online and texting friends, support and encouragement they may not be getting from their families or at school. Like straights, LGBT adults enjoy meeting each other through gay dating sites and personal ads.

Thanks to the hard work, pride, and sacrifices of gay people and gay communities of the past and present, young people today are growing up in a world where LGBT people have opportunities for full and happy lives that earlier generations could only dream of. While LGBT people still face prejudice and misunderstanding, there are many, many reasons why a young gay person should never have to feel alone, "abnormal," or hopeless. Millions of gay people have gone before them, building strong and supportive communities and fighting for their rights. A rich and diverse gay community is out there waiting to welcome a new generation, waiting to teach them and to learn from them.

FIND OUT MORE ON THE INTERNET

Gay-Straight Alliance Resources
gsanetwork.org/resources

The Human Rights Campaign
www.hrc.org

READ MORE ABOUT IT

Baima, Tracy. *Out and Proud in Chicago*. Evanston, Ill.: Surrey Books, 2008.

Goldman, Linda. *Coming Out, Coming In: Nurturing the Well-Being and Inclusion of Gay Youth in Mainstream Society.* New York: Routledge, 2008.

BIBLIOGRAPHY

The American Gay Rights Movement: A Timeline, www.infoplease.com/ipa/A0761909.html.

Belge, Kathy. "Top 5 Top Lesbian Cities in the United States." About.com Guide, lesbianlife.about.com/od/families/tp/Lesbian Cities.htm.

Duberman, Martin. *Hidden from History: Reclaiming the Gay and Lesbian Past.* Stanford, Calif.: Stanford University Press, 1990.

Faderman, Lillian. *Odd Girls and Twilight Lovers: A History of Lesbian Life in Twentieth-Century America.* New York: Penguin, 1991.

Gay-Straight Alliance Network, gsanetwork.org.

"History of the Gay Rights Movement in the US," www.lifeintheusa.com/people/gaypeople.htm.

Johnson, Ramon. "How Many Gay People Are There? Gay Population Statistics." About.com Guide, gaylife.about.com/od/comingout/a/population.htm.

Kaiser, Charles. *The Gay Metropolis: The Landmark History of Gay Life in America.* New York: Grove Press, 2007.

Katz, Jonathan. *Gay American History: Lesbians and Gay Men in the U.S.A.* New York: Harper & Row, 1985.

Lesbian, Gay, Bisexual, and Transgender Pride Month Proclamation, www.whitehouse.gov/the_press_office/Presidential-Proclamation-LGBT-Pride-Month/.

Miller, Neil. *In Search of Gay America: Women and Men in a Time of Change.* New York: Atlantic Monthly Press, 1989.

Shilts, Randy. *And the Band Played On: Politics, People, and the AIDS Epidemic.* New York: St. Martin's Press, 1987.

INDEX

AIDS 19, 29, 32–48
AIDS Coalition to Unleash Power (ACT UP) 44, 46, 48
alcohol 30, 37

Bear 49, 56–58
bohemian 27
Boystown 9–10, 16–17
Broadway 10, 17
Brokeback Mountain 25

Castro Clones 39
Castro Street 37, 48
church 10–11, 15, 25, 27, 50, 52
civil rights 32, 34, 36, 51–52, 54
college 9, 33, 36, 39–40
concentration camps 27
cowboys 25

Daughters of Bilitis (DOB) 31–32, 36
double lives 30–31

Frank, Barney 52–53

Gay and Lesbian Mardi Gras 37
gay community 18–20, 26, 28, 32, 36, 40, 42–43, 46–48, 50–51, 55, 57–58
gaydar 24

Gay Liberation Front 36
gay liberation movement 25, 28, 32, 40, 48
Gay Men's Chorus Group 10
Gay Men's Health Crisis (GMHC) 47
gay pride 10, 34, 36–37
Gay Pride Parade 34, 37
Gay-Related Immune Deficiency (GRID) 43
Gay-Straight Alliance 56
gentrification 39
Greenwich Village 27–28, 35

Human Rights Campaign 54

International Gay Rugby Association and Board (IGRAB) 56
Internet 19–20, 32, 48, 57

marriage 49, 51
Mattachine Society 32, 36
military 24, 26, 51
Milk 39
Milk, Harvey 38–39, 48, 52

Nazi 27

Obama, Barack 41, 54
oppression 13, 15, 17, 23, 37, 41

62   A New Generation of Homosexuality

Parker, Annise 52
prejudice 13, 23, 25, 28, 39, 44, 51–52, 58

Rainbow Flag 10–11
Rome 24

slang 24
social networks 19
softball 30

stereotypes 18, 39–40, 42, 52
Stonewall Inn 28, 34–35, 37
Stonewall Riots 35–36

values 13, 15

Washington Blade 46
Whitman, Walt 26
Williams Institute 17
World War II 22, 26, 32

ABOUT THE AUTHOR AND THE CONSULTANT

Bill Palmer has been involved in LGBT issues since he was Coordinator of his university's gay student alliance in the late 1970s and worked for many years for one of the largest academic publishers of LGBT books and journals in the world. Bill lives with his partner of thirty-plus years in upstate New York.

James T. Sears specializes in research in lesbian, gay, bisexual, and transgender issues in education, curriculum studies, and queer history. His scholarship has appeared in a variety of peer-reviewed journals and he is the author or editor of twenty books and is the Editor of the *Journal of LGBT Youth*. Dr. Sears has taught curriculum, research, and LGBT-themed courses in the departments of education, sociology, women's studies, and the honors college at several universities, including: Trinity University, Indiana University, Harvard University, Penn State University, the College of Charleston, and the University of South Carolina. He has also been a Research Fellow at Center for Feminist Studies at the University of Southern California, a Fulbright Senior Research Southeast Asia Scholar on sexuality and culture, a Research Fellow at the University of Queensland, a consultant for the J. Paul Getty Center for Education and the Arts, and a Visiting Research Lecturer in Brazil. He lectures throughout the world.